WITH GRATTITUDE

TO MY TEACHERS...

© 2018 Catherine Fet
North Landing Books
all rights reserved

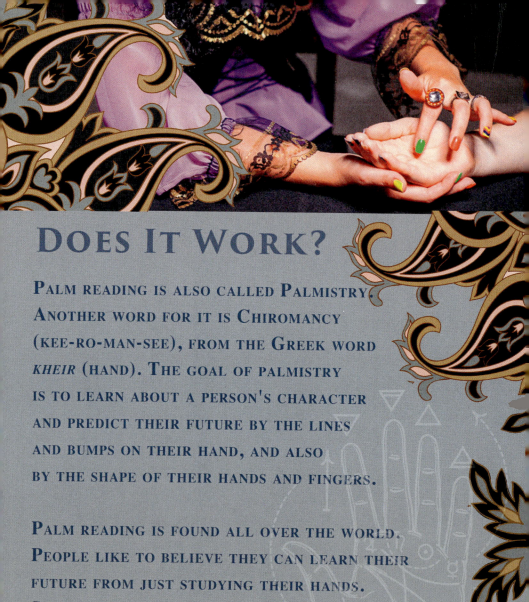

DOES IT WORK?

PALM READING IS ALSO CALLED PALMISTRY. ANOTHER WORD FOR IT IS CHIROMANCY (KEE-RO-MAN-SEE), FROM THE GREEK WORD *KHEIR* (HAND). THE GOAL OF PALMISTRY IS TO LEARN ABOUT A PERSON'S CHARACTER AND PREDICT THEIR FUTURE BY THE LINES AND BUMPS ON THEIR HAND, AND ALSO BY THE SHAPE OF THEIR HANDS AND FINGERS.

PALM READING IS FOUND ALL OVER THE WORLD. PEOPLE LIKE TO BELIEVE THEY CAN LEARN THEIR FUTURE FROM JUST STUDYING THEIR HANDS. SOUNDS A LITTLE TOO EASY, DOESN'T IT? SO IS PALM READING REAL, OR EVEN SCIENTIFIC, AS SOME PALMISTRY EXPERTS TELL US?

I DON'T HAVE AN ANSWER TO THIS QUESTION, BUT I WILL TEACH YOU PALM READING, SO YOU CAN TRY THIS MYSTERIOUS ART, ON YOUR OWN, AND REACH YOUR OWN CONCLUSION WHETHER IT'S REAL OR NOT.

FORTUNE TELLERS

Most often palm reading is done by a fortune teller. A FORTUNE TELLER is a person who claims they can predict your future and your fortune (how happy or successful you are going to be in life) by methods that have nothing to do with science, such as looking into a crystal ball, or pulling cards from a card deck, or interpreting your dreams.

They also don't like to be called fortune tellers, they prefer words that sound scientific, like: PSYCHIC (from the Greek word *PSYCHIKOS* which means *inside a person's mind*) or CLAIRVOYANT (from the French words *CLAIR*=CLEAR and *VOYANT*=SEEING) Fortune tellers are, of course, charlatans. A CHARLATAN (SHAR-LA-TAN) is a person who pretends they have a skill or knowledge in order to deceive others. But there are people who wrote books on palmistry, who studied its ancient roots, and advised kings and presidents. Do they truly know things a fortune teller doesn't know?

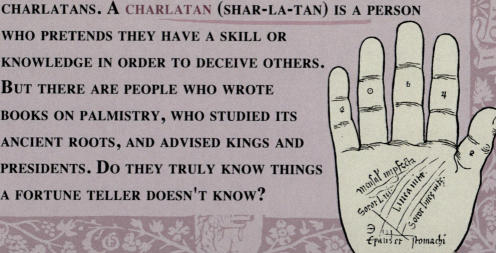

Can she predict your future? Nah.

I Promise

I can promise you one thing: By the end of this book you will know more about palmistry than any Psychic, or Clairvoyant, or Fortune Teller.

You will be able to read anyone's hand like a pro, and you will be able to practice reading the palms of your friends and family until you know for sure that palm reading really works, or that palm readers are all charlatans. (Like these two...)

Whether you believe in palm reading or not, you must promise me one thing before we start learning.

If you ever do palm reading for a friend, or a family member, or any person, you must keep everything you found out about this person SECRET.

You Promise.

Not a word to anyone ever, unless that person wants to share this information with others. It's important that people trust you, so you can practice palmistry. Some people will enjoy palm reading as a joke, but others may take it seriously, and worry that their secrets will be revealed to others. You may want to tell them at the start that you will keep everything secret forever.

The Roots of Palmistry

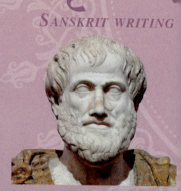

Sanskrit writing

Palmistry appeared first in ancient India. Over 3 thousand years ago, when most people on Earth didn't even have written languages, Indian palmist Valmiki wrote a book about it in Sanskrit, one of the oldest languages in the world.

From there the art of palmistry spread to China, Egypt, and Europe. Ancient Greek philosopher Aristotle (4th century B.C.) found an ancient text on palmistry and gave it as a gift to the Greek king Alexander the Great who learned to read the palms of his generals.

In the 19th century palmistry became popular in England and America when ancient Indian teachings on palm reading were discovered. Palmists claimed it was science, not just fortune telling, but scientists disagreed.

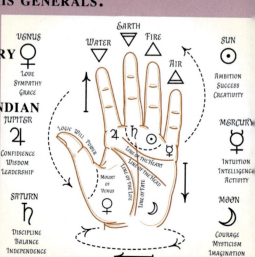

RIGHT OR LEFT?

When you do a palm reading you will study both hands. You will see that they are very much alike, but sometimes there will be differences. Here is what the Indian Palmists with whom I studied this art say about right and left hands.
One hand shows the qualities you received from your parents. The other hand shows how life changes you, and events that happen to you.

If you are a girl your right hand shows the traits from your parents. Your left hand shows your past, present and future.

If you are a boy we need to know whether you are right-handed or left-handed. Your dominant hand (the hand with which you write) will show your past, present and future.

In India, if you are a kid less than 13 years old, palmists will pay more attention to your left hand, because they believe that in kids, both boys and girls, the left hand shows more accurate information.

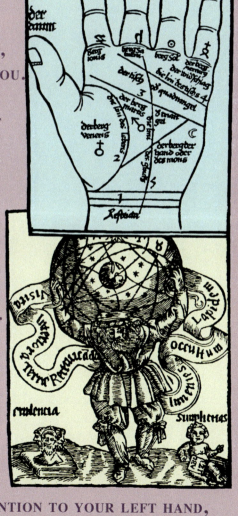

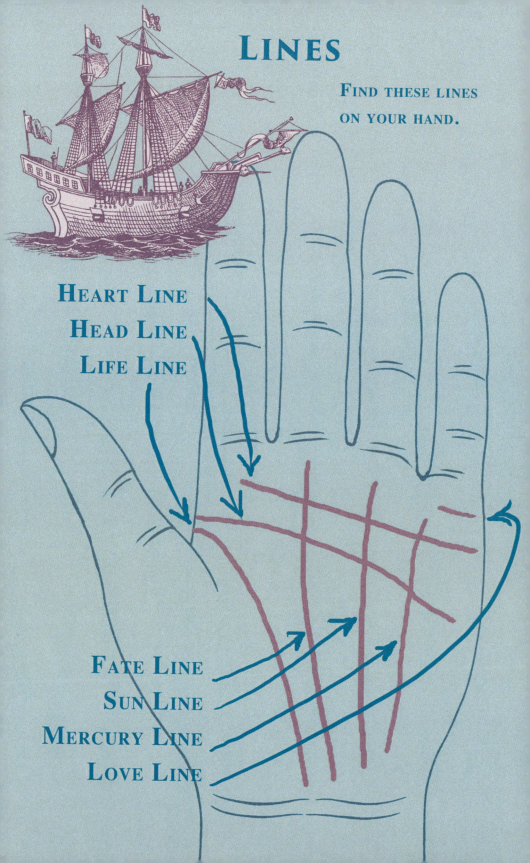

LINES

THE LIFE LINE records health and happiness. It does not predict how long you will live. The breaks in this line are times of illness or sadness.

THE HEAD LINE is strong if you are a good thinker, and good at self-control.

THE HEART LINE is deep if feelings, love, and friendship play a big role in your life.

THE FATE LINE is about your career and making money. If these are important to you, the Fate Line is long and strong.

THE SUN LINE is your talents line. It is strong if you find and grow your abilities and skills, and if people praise you for your achievements. It also shows if you are happy.

THE LOVE LINE predicts and records falling in love.

THE MERCURY LINE is about your health.

SPECIAL SIGNS

LINE BREAK: A sign of a problem or danger. But if this break is inside a square, or triangle, or there is a sister line next to it, palmists believe the break is repaired.

LINE OVERLAP: A good sign. An overlapping line is called a Sister Line. It repairs the line break.

ISLAND: A bad sign. It's either a weakness, or a loss.

SQUARE: Means protection. If your life line is broken, that means danger to your life or health. But if there is a square around the break, you are OK.

A CROSS OR CROSSBARS predict a problem or difficulty.

STAR: A sign of either great success or serious danger.

FISH: A sign of love and success.

A TRIANGLE predicts success, or talent.

TRIDENT: A sign of luck or opportunity.

FLAG: A sign a person can become well-known for their talent or great work

YOUR AGE

Palmistry divides each line on your hand into segments by age, and looks for signs on each segment to predict how well you will do throughout your life. For example, is there a crossbar on your Fate line at age 22? That may be a year of hard work and difficult decisions when you graduate from college.

Life line runs down. Fate line runs up.

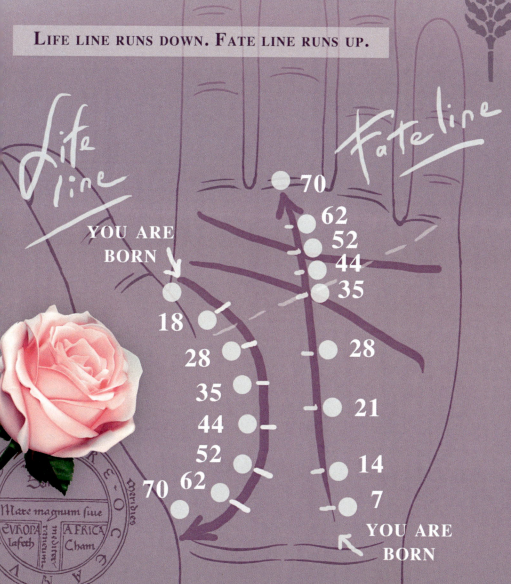

MOUNTS

Palmistry also studies the mounts, or raised areas on the palm. Are some areas on your palm higher than others? Here is what mounts mean:

Mount of Jupiter - leader and manager
Mount of Saturn - wisdom, deep knowledge
Mount of Sun - creative, artistic talents
Mount of Mercury - talent in science and business
Upper Mars - courage and fairness
Lower Mars - you want to be number 1 in everything
Mount of Venus - being loving and friendly
Mount of the Moon - imagination, creativity, charm

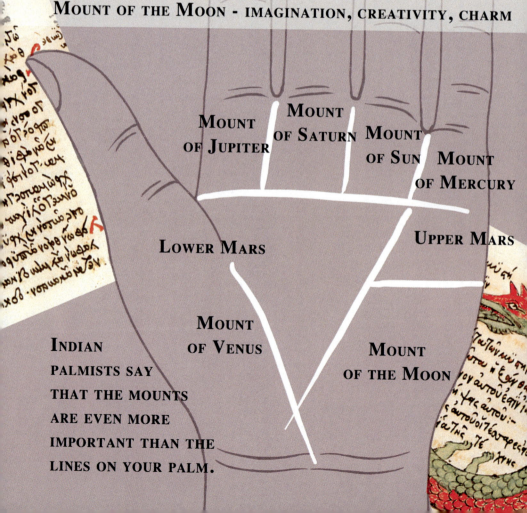

Indian palmists say that the mounts are even more important than the lines on your palm.

FINGERS

PALMISTRY SAYS THAT IF YOUR FINGERS ARE LONG, YOU HAVE PATIENCE TO GO INTO DETAILS, AND LOOK DEEP INTO PROBLEMS AND SITUATIONS.
IF YOUR FINGERS ARE SHORT, YOU ARE A FAST THINKER, BUT YOU DON'T LIKE SPENDING A LOT OF TIME SOLVING A PROBLEM.

PALMISTS ALSO DIVIDE EACH FINGER INTO 3 SEGMENTS - TOP, MIDDLE AND BOTTOM, SEPARATED BY CREASES.
IF THE LONGEST SEGMENTS OF YOUR FINGERS ARE AT THE TOP, YOU ARE A FAST LEARNER, GOOD IN SCHOOL AND LIKE WORKING WITH IDEAS, OR MAKING DISCOVERIES (A SCIENTIST, A WRITER, OR A LAWYER).
IF THE MIDDLE SEGMENT OF YOUR FINGERS IS THE LONGEST, PALMISTS SAY YOU ARE A PRACTICAL PERSON, AND YOU LIKE TO DO BUSINESS OR WORK ON SOLVING REAL WORLD PROBLEMS.
IF THE BOTTOM SEGMENT OF YOUR FINGERS IS THE LONGEST, YOU LIKE ADVENTURES, SPORTS, OR BEING OUTDOORS, LIKE HIKING IN THE MOUNTAINS, FISHING, OR SAILING.

Heart: Start and End

Indian palmistry experts say that the longer your Heart line, the better you are at understanding other people's feelings. In other words, your Heart line measures compassion. Compassion is caring about others and showing kindness.

If your Heart line starts...

- from the Mount of Jupiter, you are loving and loyal
- between the index and middle fingers, you will be happy in love and friendship because you understand people well and forgive if they hurt you.
- from the Mount of Saturn, you may sometimes find it difficult to share your thoughts and feelings.
- with a trident or a fork - great sign! It points to success on the job or in business.

Downward branches from the Heart line predict disappointments in love or friendship.

A branch that breaks your Fate line can mean that the loss of a friend may affect your career.

Head: Start and End

Palmists believe that the longer your Head line, the easier it is for you to study and learn.
If your Life line and Head line start together, you are more sensitive (your feelings are easily hurt), and the longer these lines run together, the more likely that you are defensive (you take things personally, get upset at jokes about you). If the Head line and the Life line start apart you have good self-control, good judgement, and a lot of self-confidence. If these 2 lines start far apart, you may be impulsive (act without self-control), and if the Head line ends in Upper Mars, you may take risks that get you in trouble.
If it ends in a fork, you are flexible: you can be convinced, you can change your mind.
The area between your Head and Heart lines is called the Quadrangle.
The wider this area, the more independent you are, but if it's too wide, you can make silly mistakes because you are not listening to advice.
A star in this area is a sign of success.
A triangle is a sign of patience and hard work.

Fate: Start and End

If your fate line begins...
- **on the Mount of Venus** - your family will have a strong influence on your career and success
- **from the Life line** - you will be self-made (successful on your own without anyone's help)
- **from the Head line** - the key to your success will be in your own careful planning and self-control
- **on the Mount of the Moon** - you will have success working with people. Perhaps you will be a doctor, politician, or entertainer.
- **if you don't have a Fate Line** at all this means your success will come only from your own hard work and talent, not from luck.

If your Fate line ends...
- **on the Mount of Jupiter** - you can be great in business
- **on the Mount of the Sun** - you can be a success in arts or politics.
- **with a trident on the Mount of Saturn** - great success in work and a happy family life

A triangle touching your Fate Line means luck and a great opportunity.

Mount of Jupiter
Mount of Saturn
Mount of Sun
Mount of Mercury
Lower Mars
Upper Mars
Mount of Venus
Mount of Moon
Head
Life
Fate

Sun: Start and End

If your Sun line begins...
- **on the Mount of Venus** - your family will help you find and grow your talents
- **from your Life line** - you achieve success with your own hard work and effort, not by luck
- **from the Fate line** - you will have amazing luck, or a great opportunity that you will use to succeed.
- **on the Mount of the Moon** - you have a lot of charm, people are happy to help you. This also means travel, including work in other countries.
- **on the Upper Mars** - you are competitive and good at winning

If your Sun line ends...
- **with a trident on the Mount of the Sun** - people will respect and admire you
- **with a few vertical lines on the Mount of the Sun** - you have many talents or many responsibilities
- **with a star on the Mount of the Sun** you are - or will be - a star!
- **on the Mount of Mercury** - this means lots of money!

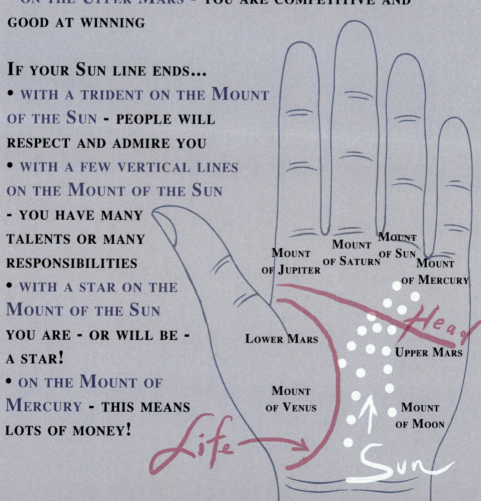

LINES PRACTICE (1)

LET'S PRACTICE USING MY HAND.

MY LIFE LINE IS DEEP AND UNBROKEN: I AM HEALTHY AND OPTIMISTIC (HOPEFUL ABOUT THE FUTURE). THERE IS AN ISLAND ON THIS LINE, BUT IT IS INSIDE A SQUARE, SO I GUESS I AM OK.
MY HEAD LINE IS LONG: I LEARN THINGS EASILY.
MY LIFE AND HEAD LINES START FAR APART, WHICH MEANS THAT I NEED TO WORK ON MY SELF-CONTROL. I CAN'T ALWAYS STOP MYSELF WHEN I AM ABOUT TO DO SOMETHING SILLY!...

HEART LINE
HEAD LINE
LIFE LINE

MY HEAD LINE IS SUPER LONG. THAT MAKES ME A PERSON WHO LIKES TO DO THINGS MY WAY - NOT ALWAYS GOOD!
MY HEART LINE STARTS BETWEEN MY INDEX AND MIDDLE FINGERS, WHICH MEANS I AM GOOD AT FINDING GREAT FRIENDS.
ALL THIS IS TRUE, WHETHER I LIKE IT OR NOT!...

ISLAND AND SQUARE   CROSSBARS

Lines Practice (2)

My FATE LINE starts on the Mount of the Moon which predicts success in public life or living abroad. It never breaks, but it gets thin near a downward branch of my Heart Line. This happens if a personal problem slows you down. That area forms a triangle - a good sign: I can overcome this problem.

My SUN LINE starts from my life line. This means that my successes in life come from my own talents and hard work, not from luck. It ends in a star! I am not into fame, but I'll take it!

Oh-oh: My Sun line is broken... Not a good sign! Maybe I missed some important opportunities.

My Mercury line (health line) is almost invisible, but Palmists say it's OK if my Fate line is strong. I also have a Mystic Cross in my Quadrangle. You find it under the Mount of Saturn and it shows interest in mystical arts like palmistry. Maybe that's why I am writing this book!

Mystic Cross
Fate line
Sun line ends in a star
Sun line broken.
Sun line starts from life line.
Love line
Mercury line

LINES PRACTICE (3)

Let's practice using my friend Katie's hand.

Katie's Life line is deep and unbroken: She is a happy person. Her Life and Head lines start together. This may mean that she is a bit sensitive. She can be upset at a silly joke, or at criticism she doesn't deserve. Her heart line is deep and starts between her index and middle fingers, which means she is a caring person and a great friend (true!) And it also has a trident on the Mount of Saturn - she is great at what she does, both on her job and for fun!
Katie's head line stops before the Upper Mars, that means she is a good team player, good at working with people.

Katie's Fate Line is broken into 3 pieces - this may be 3 different professions or living in 3 different places. There is an influence line from the Mount of the Moon breaking her Fate Line between ages 28 and 35. That can be love or a career influence.

Lines Practice (4)

Katie's Sun line starts from her heart line. Palmistry says that people with this Sun line show interest in art, music, or literature. It can also mean that Katie will discover some of her talents later in life. Also, I notice a star on Katie's Sun Line - a sign of success in creative work. Katie is an artist, and a palmist can tell this by her hand: Her Mount of Venus is raised and puffy.

Katie's fingers are longest in their middle segment. This means she is realistic. A realistic person uses their knowledge of life to make their decisions, while an idealistic person uses their imagination. Another interesting thing on Katie's hand is a cross on the Mount of Jupiter. If it is independent (not formed by lines), it means a happy marriage. But Katie is not married!... It's never too late, Katie!

Cross!
Star!
Sun Line
Heart Line
Head Line
Life Line
Mount of Venus
Mount of the Moon

LINES PRACTICE (5)

NOW LET'S PRACTICE ON MY SON'S HAND.

As I am writing this, Eric will be 7 tomorrow, so, remember, if it's a kid under 13 years old, read their left hand. Eric's Heart line starts on the Mount of Jupiter. This means he is a loyal friend you can trust.

Eric's Fate line is joined by 2 influence lines - from the Mounts of Venus and the Moon around age 21. The first one is some family influence, the second one is either living in a foreign country, or a love influence. Of course, you can't really tell at age 7. Once he is 13 we can study his right hand.

Eric's Sun line starts from his Head line. This means he will achieve success through his intelligence rather than through luck or hard work.

Heart Line
Head Line
Life Line
Mount of Jupiter
Sun line
Mount of Venus
Mount of the Moon
Influence Lines
Fate Line

LOVE LINE

The Love Line is often called the Marriage Line, but serious palmists prefer Love Line or the Line of Affection. They believe that this line records or predicts being in love and being loved, and the deeper it is the stronger the love.

A fork or an island on the Love line may point to a stressful situation between the two people, or even a breakup.

Palmists also say that if there is a vertical line coming down from your little finger and cutting the Love line, this means your family or friends may have a problem with a person you love, and maybe even try to prevent a marriage.

Love line

VERTICAL LINE

FORK

Planets and Gods (1)

In Ancient Greece and Rome they believed that planets are gods traveling across the sky. Palmistry uses these planet-god images to point to traits of a person's character.

Jupiter (Greek name, Zeus) is the king of gods, the god of law, order, and justice. In Palmistry Jupiter represents loyalty, power, self-control and good judgement.

Saturn is the god of rebirth and time. In Palmistry Saturn represents love of wisdom, study, and a peaceful personality.

Apollo (or the Sun) is the god of the arts, light, truth and inspiration. In Palmistry the Sun represents talents, magnetic personality, and being popular.

Jupiter and Apollo on Greek money

Planets and Gods (2)

Mercury (Hermes) is the god of business, diplomacy, borders and travel.
In Palmistry, Mercury represents talent or success in business, science, or public speaking.

Venus (Aphrodite) is the goddess of love and beauty.
In Palmistry Venus represents love, family, and emotions.

Mars (Ares) is the god of courage and war.
In Palmistry Mars represents courage, winning spirit, but also conflict.

Diana (Artemis), or the Moon, is the goddess of freedom and protection.
In Palmistry the Moon represents imagination, creative talents, love of change, and travel.

Planet Symbols

Palmistry, like astronomy and astrology uses special symbols for planets or areas on your hand. These are the symbols of Greek Gods whose names were given to planets.

♃	**Jupiter** - a thunderbolt or an eagle
♄	**Saturn** - a sickle (a harvesting tool)
☉	**Sun** - a sun disk
☿	**Mercury** - a winged helmet and a staff
♀	**Venus** - a hand mirror
♂	**Mars** - a shield and a spear
☾	**Moon** - a crescent

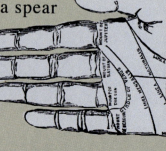

UPSIDE DOWN?

When you study palmistry, you start by looking at your own hands, so all the pictures in this book show hands with fingers up, the way you see your own hand.

But real professional palmists always sit opposite the person whose palm they read, and they see their hands upside down, the fingers pointing down. It's OK to sit side-by-side when you are learning palm reading, but if you want to look like a real palmistry expert, you will need to get used to looking at people's hands upside down. You may also need a good magnyfying glass!

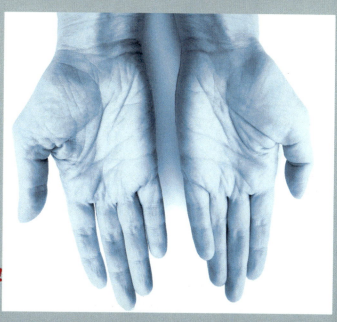

Palmistry Journal

As you learn palm reading, it is very useful to be able to compare different hands. I suggest that you start your own palmistry journal where you keep pictures of the hands you have read, and your thoughts and predictions about each hand. Can you imagine reading your predictions 20 years later? Wow!

Ask permission to take pictures of people's hands, have them printed out, glue it into your journal and write your comments and predictions.

My Indian teachers used to cover hands with paint and make hand prints on paper for their journals, but they learned palmistry in the days when there were no phones with cameras and no printers! I thought it would be fun to do hand printing, so I tried it. It was a disaster! I hadn't done it since I was in pre-K!.. So, take pictures and have your family print them out!

PALMISTRY CHARTS (1)

HERE IS HOW PALMISTS OF THE MIDDLE AGES AND LATER TIMES DREW HAND CHARTS IN THEIR PALMISTRY JOURNALS AND IN TEXTBOOKS.

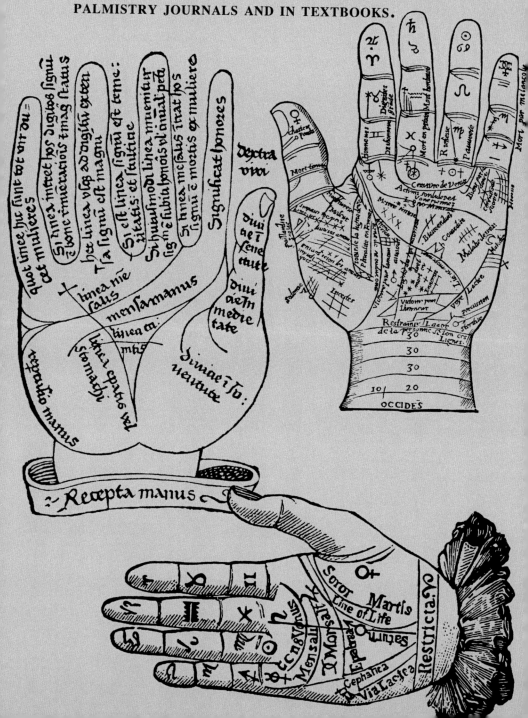

Palmistry Charts (2)

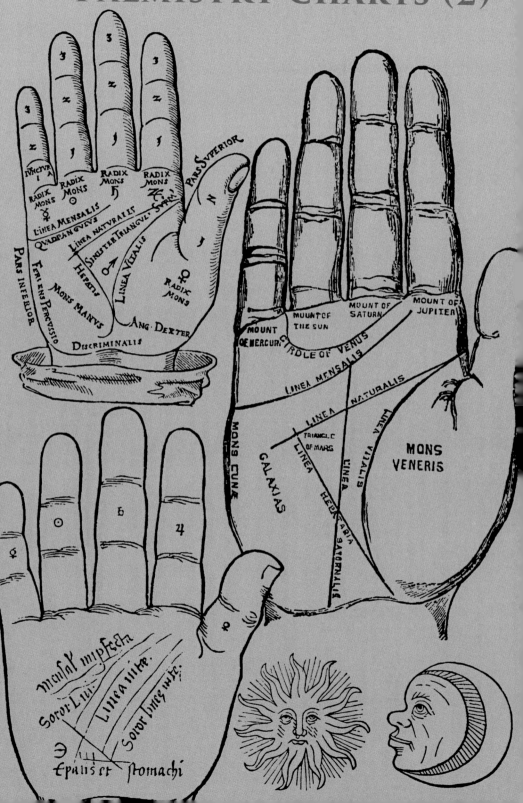

WRONG!

Here are a few examples of wrong predictions often made by fortune tellers. Now that you know a lot about palmistry, we can laugh together at these ideas:

• The longer your Life Line, the longer you will live.

• The longer the Fate Line the better you will do in your profession.

• If your Love Line is close to the Heart Line, you will get married early.

• If you have a few parallel lines instead of one Love Line, you will be married a few times.

• Vertical lines cutting your Love Line show the number of children you will have (thick lines - boys, thin lines - girls!)

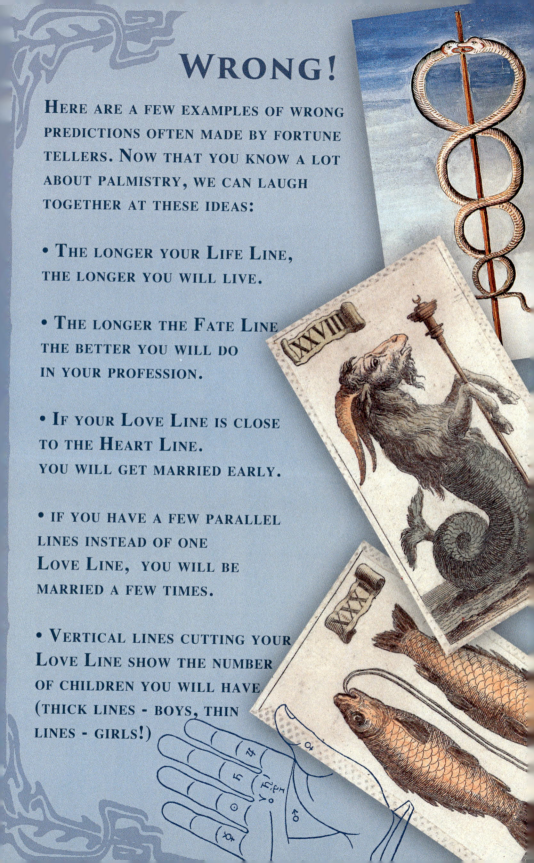

Charlatan Tricks

Most fortune tellers do not know palmistry, but they act like they do and people believe them. How do they do this?

1. They say things that happen to everyone and claim they can see it on your hand. Everyone is stressed, or disappointed, or hopeful at some point. The fortune teller says: *I see you had a disappointment last year.* Well, once a year a disappointment will happen to anyone! Or they say: *I see a great opportunity for you...* But there are opportunities in every person's future!

2. They look for cues in your body language. If you lean forward listening to them, they know that you want to believe them. If you nod, if your eyes open wider, or you stop smiling, they know they just said something that you believe is true.

3. They make you tell them what you want to hear. They'll say, *Your hand tells me someone in your family is very unhappy with you.* You stop smiling. They know it happened to you. Well, everyone has family trouble from time to time. They continue, *But there will be an opportunity to make peace real soon...* You start smiling again. Now they know what you want to hear and why you came to them!

WHAT IS BODY LANGUAGE?

Body language is how you say things without using words. Body language is:

1. **Your facial expression**: Are you smiling or frowning?
2. **Your gestures** (what you do with your hands - pointing, touching your face, crossing your arms)
3. **Your voice**: Is it high or low, are you talking slowly or quickly?
4. **Your eye movements**: Are you making eye contact (looking someone in the eye), looking away or down? Maybe you roll your eyes or blink a lot.
5. **Your breath** (breathing fast, or holding your breath)
6. **Your posture** (how you hold your body - your back straight, your chin up, or your back bent, chin down).
7. **Your personal space** - are yoy standing close to a person you are talking to, or keeping your distance?
8. **Touch**: Do you give someone a hug, touch their hand, slap them on the shoulder or back?

So if your eyes grow big, your mouth opens, your eyebrows jump up and you bring your hands to your face, most likely you are surprised, and maybe even a little scared!

BODY LANGUAGE EXAMPLES

THINKING OR WONDERING
LOOKING UP
TOUCHING HIS CHIN
HEAD TILTED

NERVOUS OR GUILTY
LOOKING DOWN
SHOULDERS DOWN
ARMS PRESSED TO THE BODY

WORRYING OR SCARED
FROWNING
LOOKING SIDEWAYS
SHUOLDERS UP
TOUCHING FACE

FRUSTRATED, TRYING TO REMEMBER
SQUINTING
FINGER SNAPPING
BENT FORWARD

WARNING
TURNING TO THE SIDE, CHIN DOWN
POINTING FINGER
LIPS PRESSED TOGETHER

UPSET, FRUSTRATED
FROWNING
HEAD TILTED
FIST CLENCHED
ARMS CROSSED

Bad Reputation

People have always suspected that fortune tellers were dishonest. Here is a painting from 1630 by the French artist Georges de La Tour *The Fortune Teller*. Take a close look!

A young man came to a fortune teller. While she reads his palm and takes a coin he paid her, look what her friends are doing:
One is stealing the young man's coin purse!
The other one is ready to grab it!
The third one is cutting off his gold chain!

BELIEVE IT OR NOT!

Some people believe in palmistry, astrology, or other arts that are not scientific, and others don't. It's important that we respect both, those who do and those who don't, and never laugh at people for their beliefs.

It's good to be **open-minded**. An open-minded person says: *I don't know if what you believe in is true or not, but I will listen to what you have to say.* The opposite is a narrow-minded person who thinks that if you don't share their beliefs, you are stupid or evil.

It's also good to be **tolerant**. A tolerant person doesn't make you feel uncomfortable, even if they disagree with your beliefs. If you say something they think is silly, they will smile and say nothing. But if you meet an intolerant person, they will demand that you agree with them, and if you still disagree, they won't be friends with you.

Another good rule is *Don't judge*. We all have something in our beliefs or behavior that can make people think we are funny, or silly, or not grownup. We can't all laugh at each other! Better to ignore the differences and be friends. I have friends with whom I disagree on a lot of things, but I never argue with them. Friendship is more important to me than winning an argument.

Made in the USA
Las Vegas, NV
01 December 2022